A Walk Through the Dark

nephertiri belcher

BookLeaf Publishing

India | USA | UK

Presentation by *BookLeaf Publishing*

Web: www.bookleafpub.com

E-mail: info@bookleafpub.com

ISBN: 9789358313079

First edition 2024

I would like to dedicate this book to all the people, who like myself, have walked through the dark.

Self harm

But you tried already and it didn't work

But it's ok

They don't need to know the chinks In your armor

Because you wear those scars like armor that will never break

Your emotionThey don't the relief that is taking a pill or putting a blade to your arm

They tell you that you need to shut up and deal with it

They tell you that other people have it worse than you and your over reacting

But as soon as they see those burn marks or scars they ask why hadn't you told them your hurting
The act of doing something that someone else thinks hurts you

The act of trying to relieve pain that someone so
happen to say was harmful

But they don't know

They don't know the constant pain weighing you
down like a ton of cinder blocks

The sinking feeling every time you look in the
mirror

They don't know the effort it takes to get out of
bed in the morning

But that's ok

It's ok that they don't know what we're going
through

It's ok that they assume it hurts

But they don't know

Why didn't you come to them

Why, why, why

s and heart protected behind a shield of false
happiness

Sadness

I see a dark room
It's cold but not freezing

I don't know how long It's been like this
Or if there is anything else

But when I concentrate
All I can see is a faint wisp of color

It's dark; I'm tired
But I know I can't sleep
I don't know what will happen if I do

It's back again

Anxiety

Heart racing

Ears ringing

It's just school

It's just people

It's just a conversation

Repeating that
it will be fine and it's not that a big of a deal

It will be alright

Your heart isn't beating out of your chest
You're not hyperventilating

You're just nervous

Nightmares

Waking up in the middle of the night

Shaking and hyperventilating

Not knowing what's going on

Thinking that something terrible happened

But realizing it was all in your head

Loss

My hands feel cold without you here
My heart feels empty while you're gone
For you are my everything
And with you gone
I am nothing

Silent Anger

Being so mad that you stay silent

Voice caught in your throat

Tears of anger running down your face

Being so mad you can't even yell or scream

Silence

Sitting alone in complete silence

Surrounded by nothing but quiet

The silence louder then any object or person
could ever be

Drowning in your own thoughts and fears

Drowning in silence

Numbness

How funny

I used to Hope

To feel

Nothing

When I was in pain

But now,
That i don't feel anything

I realize that

Being in pain
Is better than being numb

Suicide

Death is scary

But the pain and sorrow of living is too much

Waking up, getting out of bed, talking to people
It's all too much
Too stressful

So Being dead is better than being in a place you
don't belong
Surrounded by people that hurt you

Gaslighting

It isn't real

It isn't real

It isn't real

It isn't real

It isn't real

It isn't real

It isn't real

You're going crazy.

Total isolation

Being around people
Is exhausting

Hearing them laugh and talk
Speak about random things and laughing at
jokes

It's annoying,
Upsetting and most of all it hurts

It hurts to see other people being happy
Having fun,

While your alone, by yourself
Isolated in your own little world

Knowing that you won't get to laugh or have fun
with others because they might hurt you in the
end

Hate

You hurt me
But I still love you
You lie to me
But I still love you
You ignore me
But I still love you

I forgave you
So many times

I helped you
As much as I could

So I don't understand
How my love
Turned into hate

Being lost

I don't know
I don't know where to go
I don't know what to do
I don't know what to think
For I am lost
Without the guidance of another

Disappointment

Nothing hurts more then
Disappointing the person you look up to
The person you never want to hurt
And the pain of knowing
You let them down

Jealousy

Sometimes,
I am jealous of the birds
Because they are far more free
Then I could ever be

Memories

When I think of you
I remember your smile
I remember your laugh
And then
I remember that
I won't be able to see your smile again

Growing up

Growing up is seeing
Seeing all the things you have been oblivious to

Growing up is realizing
Realizing that not everything has a happy ending

Its realizing that the line between
Being oblivious and being hopeful
Is almost invisible

That is the reality of growing up

Ruthlessness

The world is cruel
It will take advantage of you
It will break you
It will swallow you whole

In a world without mercy
You have to be ruthless

Because ruthlessness
Is mercy upon ourselves